EAST ANGLIAN BUSES SINCE 1990

EAST ANGLIAN BUSES SINCE 1990

DAVID MOTH

AMBERLEY

First published 2018

Amberley Publishing
The Hill, Stroud
Gloucestershire, GL5 4EP

www.amberley-books.com

Copyright © David Moth, 2018

The right of David Moth to be identified as
the Author of this work has been asserted in
accordance with the Copyrights, Designs and
Patents Act 1988.

ISBN 978 1 4456 8352 2 (print)
ISBN 978 1 4456 8353 9 (ebook)

British Library Cataloguing in Publication Data.
A catalogue record for this book is available from
the British Library.

Origination by Amberley Publishing.
Printed in the UK.

Introduction

This book, covering East Anglian buses, straddles the last years of the twentieth century along with the first fifteen of the twenty-first, with the most recent images taken in 2015. I have found it a difficult task to whittle the images down to a final 180 and I have tried hard not to let one area or operator be over-represented. Therefore, this is I hope a reasonable representation of the bus scene over the period covered in this book.

When compiling this book I researched what actually constitutes East Anglia. There doesn't seem to be any legal definition of East Anglia, nor does there seem to be any kind of general consensus, so I've included what would be my general interpretation of East Anglia, that being the counties of Norfolk, Suffolk, Cambridgeshire and the northern half of Essex. There is one photograph taken in Oundle in the easternmost corner of Northamptonshire, but I hope I can be forgiven for that as it features a Peterborough-based Bristol Lodekka having a rare outing in normal service.

One major operator some readers may consider conspicuous by its almost complete absence is the Chelmsford-based former Tilling/NBC company Eastern National. This is simply down to the fact that almost all of my best Eastern National images are included in my book *Eastern National: The Final Years*, so I considered it would be poor value for buyers of this book if I were to repeat those images in this collection.

During most of the period covered by this collection of images I lived in Cherry Hinton on the edge of Cambridge, then Braintree in the north of Essex. So while I have striven to cover the area reasonably uniformly, it is probably inevitable that a high proportion of photographs will be taken in Cambridge and Braintree.

The photographs in this book are arranged chronologically, so as the reader leafs through it they will observe the vehicle types and liveries gradually change.

Of course, in 1990 there was no such thing as low-floor buses and they gradually start creeping into the images in this book from 1996 onwards with a photograph of Stagecoach Cambus Dennis Dart 364 P564 EFL. It was the first low-floor bus I ever rode on and I remember being impressed by the wide, low entrance, mainly as the bus was full and I was unable to find a seat, meaning I had to stand near the front of the bus, allowing me plenty of time to look at it. By 2015 almost all buses were low-floor and it was difficult to find a bus with a step entrance still in service, although right at the end of the book there is a photograph of a Hedingham Volvo Olympian taken in its last few months of service in October 2015.

This book also covers the gradual disappearance of the Cambus and Eastern Counties liveries and the replacement liveries of the groups they were absorbed into. By sheer luck I happened to photograph Leyland Olympian H474 CEG in three different liveries during its life with Viscount and later Stagecoach. I had no idea that I had until I started compiling images for this book.

While I have tried to include a general representation of bus operations in this area during the period covered by this book it is inevitable that one or two areas of interest to some people would be left out. There are also very few minibus images, apart from Cambus Optare MetroRiders, as to me they were simply not of interest.

I do hope you enjoy looking through this collection as much as I enjoyed compiling it. I have endeavoured to keep all dates and captions as accurate as possible.

Cambus Volkswagen LT55 Optare CityPacer 922 (E42 RDW) is seen in Cambridge city centre loading with passengers for the City Rail Link in July 1990.

Eastern Counties Leyland Olympian/Northern Counties F105 AVG is seen in Peterborough bus station waiting to depart on the trunk route 794 to Norwich via King's Lynn. The coach seats made these buses quite suited for this lengthy route. Under First Group ownership this route was renumbered X1 and extended to Lowestoft via Great Yarmouth, though it has since been cut back to Norwich and rebranded Excel. July 1990.

In 1989 Cambus created the Viscount subsidiary for the operations around the Peterborough area. Seen in July 1990 is open-top Bristol FLF JAH 552D on the shuttle service from Peterborough to the East of England Show. Note that it is carrying its original Eastern Counties fleetnumber of FLF452.

Also seen at the East of England Show in July 1990 is Viscount semi-preserved Bristol FLF JAH 553D. At the time in a red livery, it is also wearing its original fleetnumber. Both of these vehicles are still owned by Stagecoach.

In the autumn of 1990, Hedingham Bedford YMQ L1245 (FCY 293W) is seen in Parkway in Chelmsford on the Essex County Council-contracted route 52 from Pleshey. The 52 was operated by Eastern National for decades but was not registered by EN at the time of deregulation. Upon deregulation the route was altered to run via Springfield and was operated by Hedingham.

Eastern National only ever bought one small batch of four Bristol LHs and they didn't last long in the fleet before being sold to Hedingham. L111 (UVX 4S) is seen in Braintree Bus Park on 17 April 1991.

Series 2 Bristol VRTs had a long life with Eastern Counties. VR143 (GNG 709N) is seen in Stowmarket on 16 August 1991.

Eastern Counties had a huge fleet of Bristol VRTs. In the early 1980s, under NBC ownership, they weren't keen on the newly launched Leyland Olympian, so took the opportunity to buy several VRTs during the type's final year of existence. VR242 (JAH 242V) is seen at Ipswich bus station on 16 August 1991, with the Buttermilk Centre going up in the background.

VR243 (JAH 243V) is seen entering Ipswich bus station on 13 August 1992, with the completed Buttermilk Centre visible behind it.

Also taken on 13 August 1992 is this photograph of Eastern Counties Bristol VRT VR185 (ODL 658R), which was new to Southern Vectis as 658 in 1977 and sold to Eastern Counties in 1991. Seen in Sudbury bus station, it is about to return to its home town of Ipswich.

Chambers Leyland Lynx E87 KGV is seen in Sudbury on the local service to Cornard Estate on 13 August 1992.

ECW-bodied Leyland Atlanteans were the backbone of the Colchester Borough Transport fleet for several years. 85 (MEV 85V) is seen at Chelmsford railway station in January 1993, shortly before Colchester Council sold the municipality to British Bus.

United Counties was fairly unusual in that it was sold directly to one of the emerging big groups when it was privatised, in this case Stagecoach. Bristol VRT 862 (RRP 862R) is seen missing its front grill when leaving Cambridge bus station on 28 January 1993. This was towards the end of the time when Stagecoach subsidiaries had individual styles of fleetnames.

Also seen in Cambridge on 28 January 1993 is Whippet open-top Metropolitan WKH 426S, which is being used as a single-decker with the top deck closed off and covered with tarpaulin.

About a year into ownership by the British Bus Group, Colchester Borough Transport Atlantean 75 (TPU 75R) is seen in Colchester High Street on 29 April 1994.

For several years Cedric's Coaches ran local bus services between Colchester and Brightlingsea via Wivenhoe in competition with Eastern National. Bristol VRT WWY 120S was new to West Yorkshire and was owned and operated in southern Essex for a short while with Stephensons of Rochford before being sold on to Cedric's. Seen in Wivenhoe en route to Brightlingsea on 29 April 1994, it is not actually displaying a route number, but is probably on the 78X.

Osbornes OSR 191R is seen in Maldon on 16 May 1994. One of twenty-five Bristol VRTs with Alexander bodywork bought by Tayside Regional Council in 1977, these buses didn't last long in Scotland and were sold on to various English operators. Osbornes of Tollesbury purchased this solitary example from Tayside in 1980 and it had a long life with this Essex independent, lasting until Osbornes was taken over by Hedingham in 1997.

One of a large batch of Leyland Olympians with Northern Counties bodies purchased new by Cambus, 517 (F517 NJE) is seen in Ely on 24 May 1994 in what turned out to be the final version of Cambus livery before CHL Holdings was taken over by Stagecoach the following year.

One of several Metrobuses that London Buses leased for its Harrow Buses operation, E455 SON is seen in Caistor on 8 Friday 1994. When the lease expired in 1991, these buses, with several years of useful life left in them, were snapped up by many operators, including council-owned Great Yarmouth Transport.

By 1995 Whippet was the only operator still using Metropolitans in passenger service, all of which were second-hand. The type was notorious for corrosion, although in fairness it paved the way for the very successful Metrobus. New to London Transport as MD 123, OUC 123R is seen in Cambridge city centre in May 1995 having worked in on the 1A from Huntingdon (although no route number is visible).

Leyland Lynx F168 SMT was one of a pair acquired along with the Millerbus fleet by Cambus. Now very much part of the Cambus fleet, numbered 311, it is seen on its usual haunt at the time, the Park and Ride service, in May 1995.

Cambus inherited several Bristol VRTs from Eastern Counties upon the latter's partition in 1984. Seen about to enter Cambridge bus station in May 1995 is 703 (NAH 138P), which was new to Eastern Counties in 1976.

In 1993 Cambus purchased fourteen Volvo B6s with locally built Marshall bodywork – a combination that I believe was unique to Cambus. 162 (L662 MFL) is seen on the 4 to Colville Estate in the village suburb of Cherry Hinton. Colville Estate is no longer served by buses at the time of writing.

One of three B6s in the City Rail link livery, 169 (L669 MFL) is seen turning out of Emmanuel Road into Parker Street in Cambridge city centre during the mini heatwave of May 1995.

Coach-seated Leyland Olympian 500 (E500 LFL) is seen in Cambridge in May 1995.

Viscount Bristol VRT SUB 793W is seen departing Wisbech bus station on Saturday 27 May 1995. This bus is now preserved.

This Emblings AEC Reliance is seen near March railway station on Saturday 27 May 1995.

Looking very smart in Emblings livery is ex-Aberdeen Corporation Transport 132 (PRG 132J), which was reregistered 3196 DD and then OFL 113J. A Daimler Fleetline with an Alexander body, this bus was new in February 1971. Seen on Saturday 27 May 1995, this bus was withdrawn by January 1996 and used as spares.

Another Bristol VRT inherited from Eastern Counties was Cambus Bristol VRT 712 (OPW 182P), which is seen in Millerbus livery in Cambridge in June 1995.

Cambus Leyland Olympian/Roe 505 (UWW 8X) is seen resting on the roundabout on Gazelle Way in June 1995. Not long after I took this photograph the land behind the roundabout was acquired by Tesco's and a superstore exists there now, opened in 1997. This bus was new to West Yorkshire PTE as 5008 in March 1982. It was then sold off lease to Cambus in March 1987, to Fleetlink of Liverpool in March 2001 and then to Williams of Oadby in April 2001.

Cambus had a sizable fleet of Optare MetroRiders, which it used on Cambridge city services. 969 (K969 HUB) is seen in the Chesterton area in July 1995.

Stagecoach United Counties Bristol VRT 903 (CBD 903T) is seen in Cambridge in July 1995. The large local fleetnames would soon be removed from Stagecoach group vehicles, being replaced with the new style, with the name of the local fleet secondary to the Stagecoach name.

Bristol VRT STW 30W was new to Eastern National in 1981 as a seventy-seat bus. Passing to Thamesway in 1990, it was sold to Greens of Kirkintilloch in May 1991 only to find its way back down south in October of that year when it was bought by Cambus. In December 1996 it was sold on to Hedingham, where it spent four years before being sold for preservation. At the time of writing I believe it is painted into London Transport livery and is the property of a school in London.

Cambus Volvo B6 163 (L663 MFL) is captured in Cherry Hinton High Street on 14 July 1995. Cherry Hinton officially became part of Cambridge in 1934.

Cambus Volvo B6 163 is seen again, this time in Mill Road in the Romsey Town area of Cambridge on 5 August 1995.

Cambus Leyland Olympian 503 (UWW 3X) is seen on Gazelle Way in Cherry Hinton in August 1995 on its usual haunt, the 5 from Cherry Hinton to Arbury. At the time four buses carried route branding for the 5 – three Olympians and one VRT, although in the case of the latter the route branding was only carried on the windscreen of the bus.

Osborne's Leyland Leopard EWW 213T is seen at Witham Safeway's (now a Morrisons) on Saturday 10 February 1996. Osborne's would soon be sold to Hedingham.

Carrying the new style of fleetname, United Counties Bristol VRT FRP 910T is seen at Huntingdon bus depot (since demolished) on 14 February 1996 in the company of a couple of Volvo B6s.

The first of three pictures of Leyland Olympian H474 CEG in as many liveries, it is seen here in Viscount livery on 14 February 1996. The CHL group, of which Viscount was a subsidiary, was taken over by Stagecoach on 7 December 1995.

Also taken on 14 February 1996 is this picture of Viscount Bristol VRT VAH 279X. For some time these buses would not display any sign of the change of ownership.

Eastern Counties was taken over by GRT Holdings in 1994 and GRT merged with Badgerline Holdings in 1995 to form FirstBus. Full-height Bristol VRT series 2 VR334 (KKE 734N), new to Maidstone & District, is seen in King's Lynn bus station on 15 February 1996.

Cambus Volvo B6s 167 and 168 are seen at Cambridge station on the City Rail Link on Saturday 17 February 1996.

Stagecoach Cambus Mercedes 206 (N616 VSS) in Cambridge when virtually brand new on 26 February 1996.

New to London Transport as MD 109, Whippet Metropolitan OUC 109R is seen departing Cambridge bus station for Huntingdon on 26 February 1996. By 1996 Metropolitans were extremely rare.

Eastern Counties Leyland National 592 (WAH 592S) is seen in King's Lynn loading for the 411 to Hunstanton on 1 March 1996.

Two Eastern Counties Bristol VRTs from the same batch line up for an interesting comparison of liveries. DEX 236T is still in the deregulation 'Post Office red' livery, while DEX 229T is in the newer GRT style livery. Note the upper-deck front windows have been replaced with non-opening ones. This was common on surviving VRTs by the mid-1990s.

Eastern Counties Mercedes Minibus N616 GAH is seen in King's Lynn on 1 March 1996.

Eastern Counties Dennis Lance K739 KAH is seen in King's Lynn bus station on 1 March 1996.

New to Ribble in 1972, Eastern Counties 315 (OCK 985K) is a very early series 2 Bristol VRT and was a very rare survivor by 13 March 1996, when this photograph was taken in Lowestoft. This bus was withdrawn in April of that year and is now preserved in NBC livery by the East Anglian Transport Museum in Carlton Colville.

Eastern Counties Bristol VRT 313 (CJO 470R) is seen in Norwich on 19 April 1996. Note it retains its original upper-deck front windows. This bus was new to Oxford South Midland.

FirstBus transferred a few Bristol VRTs with East Lancs bodies from Northampton Transport to Eastern Counties in 1996. ABD 72X is seen in Norwich on 19 April 1996.

Eastern Counties Bristol VRT 193 (TEX 403R) is seen in Norwich on 19 April 1996. Very few VRTs would be seen in the GRT style livery while retaining their original front upper-deck windows. For a while I believed this was the only one. Note the 'Welcome to FirstBus' window etching in the lower-deck window.

Colchester Borough Transport Leyland Atlantean 78 (VNO 78S) is seen in Colchester bus station on 8 July 1996. It is interesting to note that by the time I took this picture CBT had been a subsidiary of British Bus plc for three years, but there was no sign on the bus of the change of ownership. In August 1996 British Bus was taken over by the Cowie Group.

Morley's Bristol VRT/Northern Counties NDP 38R is seen in Peterborough bus station on 19 August 1996. This bus was new to Reading Transport, where the type were known as Jumbos. It is now preserved.

Stagecoach Cambus Dennis Dart 364 (P564 APM) entered service on 1 August 1996 and was mainly used at first on route 5, the cross-city route. This was the first Dennis Dart to enter service with Stagecoach Cambus, although it would be joined by three others in May 1997. It was very unusual at the time for a Stagecoach Dennis Dart to have Plaxton bodywork. It is seen in August 1996 in Cambridge, and note the nonstandard application of Stagecoach livery.

Stagecoach Cambus Volvo B6 158 (L658 MFL) leads a line up of three buses on city services on 9 October 1996. This picture demonstrates how the fleet was undergoing repainting at the time.

Carters Bristol RE SVW 274K (new to Eastern National) is seen departing Colchester bus station on the Essex County Council-contracted 750 to Brantham on Friday 24 January 1997. This bus is now preserved in EN livery.

Stagecoach Cambus Volvo B6 161 (L661 MFL) is still in Cambus livery when seen in Bridewell Road, Cherry Hinton, in July 1997. My 1973 Ford Cortina 2000 GXL is parked behind. Although I parted with the Cortina in 1999, I believe at the time of writing it does still survive.

Stagecoach Cambus Optare MetroRider 971 (K971 HUB) is still in the attractive Cambus livery when seen in Cherry Hinton in July 1997.

Stagecoach Dennis Dart 324 (P324 EFL) was one of three Darts that joined the fleet in May 1997 and was mainly used at first on the 5, ousting the double-deckers that previously worked the route. It is seen here in Cambridge on 9 October 1997.

Stagecoach Cambus Optare MetroRider 963 (K963 HUB) is seen at Cambridge bus station on 12 November 1997, blinded for the 44 to Fulbourn. This was an old Premier Travel route, and one that would be extended to Haverhill, although that would prove to be short-lived.

Stagecoach Cambus Iveco Daily K173 CAV is seen in Cambridge in January 1998.

Eastern Counties Bristol VRT 223 (BVG 223T) is seen at Heartsease Roundabout, Norwich, on 3 February 1998. I always think Bristol VRTs look odd without foglamps.

Eastern Counties Dennis Dart 421 (K741 JAH) is seen in Park and Ride livery on route 20 in Norwich on 3 February 1998.

Eastern Counties Mercedes 901 (D758 LEX) is seen in Castle Meadow, Norwich, on 19 March 1998.

First Eastern Counties Dennis Dart R461 BNG is seen on 18 March 1998.

First Eastern Counties Dennis Javelin 506 (G706 JAH) is seen in Norwich on the X58 to Sheringham on 18 March 1998.

169 (L669 MFL) is seen at Showbus at Duxford on 27 September 1998. That year Stagecoach Cambus repainted the Volvo B6s used on the City Rail Link service into this striking livery. This livery proved to be short-lived as not long after improvements to the frequencies of other city routes led the Rail Link service to be withdrawn.

First Eastern Counties Leyland Olympian 103 (XHK 237X) is seen at Thorpeness on 14 August 1999. This early Olympian was one of a batch of three that were new to Eastern National in 1981. They first passed to Thamesway before being transferred by FirstBus to Eastern Counties.

First Eastern Counties Leyland National 1770 (XNG 770S) is seen in King's Lynn on 8 January 1999.

First Eastern Counties Dennis Javelin 512 (H612 RAH) is seen in Saxmundham on 25 March 1999.

Hedingham Omnibus Leyland Tiger L269 (GVS 948Y) is seen on one of the routes that came with the recently purchased Osborne's business in Colchester on 24 March 1998.

Hedingham Omnibus Bristol VRT L194 (JWV 271W) is seen at Kelvedon Depot on 18 September 1999. By this time Hedingham's VRTs were mainly used on school duties.

In the late 1990s, Arriva transferred several Metrobuses to its Colchester fleet to replace the Leyland Atlanteans with more modern buses (although it's fair to point out that the Metrobuses weren't much newer than the buses they replaced and indeed the oldest Metrobuses were in fact older than some of the newer Atlanteans). New to London Transport as M410, 5350 (GYE 410W) is seen entering Colchester High Street on 22 April 2000.

Ipswich Buses commemorated the withdrawal of their last Leyland Atlanteans with a running day on Saturday 30 September 1999; 35 (SDX 35R) is seen in Ipswich town centre on that day. This bus is now preserved.

Also seen on 30 September 2000 is Ipswich Buses Leyland Atlantean 32 (SDX 32R).

A much newer member of the Ipswich Buses fleet is Dennis Dart 91 (X91 LBJ), also seen on 30 September 2000.

On the same day, First Eastern Counties Scania L94 is also seen in Ipswich.

One of several Volvo Olympians transferred by Stagecoach from its London fleets to Cambridge, P807 GMU is seen here still in LT red in the spring of 2001 in Cherry Hinton.

Stagecoach Cambus Volvo B6 (L456 YAC) is seen at Cambridge railway station in the spring of 2001. This bus saw further service with Whippet.

First Eastern Counties Bristol VRT 304 (PRC 850X), formerly of Trent, is seen in Colchester bus station on 7 March 2001 in the Eastern Counties version of the livery First introduced for its East Anglian fleets.

First Eastern National Bristol VRT 3083 (STW 27W) stands in Chelmsford bus station alongside Arriva Dennis Dart K321 CVX in May 2001.

Stagecoach Cambus Volvo Olympian 541 (P541 EFL) clearly has a malfunctioning destination display when seen here departing Cambridge station in August 2001. This large batch of Olympians was leased by Stagecoach for its Cambus and Viscount fleets, and when the lease expired they found new homes throughout the country.

One of a few Dennis Darts transferred into the Cambus fleet, L756 VNL is seen at Cambridge station in August 2001. This location has changed tremendously in recent years.

Cambus Leyland Olympian 503 (UWW 3X) was the first of the Cambus fleet to acquire Stagecoach livery in January 1996. It is seen here at Cambridge station on 25 August 2001.

Hedingham Volvo B6 L208 (L208 RNO) is seen at Colchester bus station on 2 January 2002.

First Eastern Counties Dennis Dart 415 (L501 VHU) is seen in Norwich on 13 April 2002 with route branding for the 25 while working on the 18.

First Eastern Counties Scania L94 is seen in green Park and Ride livery on 15 April 2002.

Guide Friday MCW MetroRider F60 RFS is seen on the commercially operated 007 in Cambridge in August 2001.

Stagecoach Cambus Volvo Olympian P575 EFL is seen at the Grafton Centre bus stops in Cambridge on the 77 Park and Ride on 15 April 2002.

Stagecoach Bristol FLF JAH 553D is seen on the East of England shuttle service while wearing a Golden Jubilee Stagecoach livery on 15 June 2002.

I now regret displaying the date on the image when I was using this camera, especially when it kept going wrong and resetting itself like it did here. Whippet Leyland Titan KYV 346X is seen departing Cambridge bus station while heading for St Ives in the spring of 2003, probably on the 1A, although Whippet buses at the time often didn't display route numbers.

Here we see Leyland Olympian H474 CEG for the second time in this book. Now wearing Stagecoach stripes and renumbered 14524, it is seen in Cambridge in the spring of 2003 on the 155 to St Ives, despite displaying Cambridge in the windscreen.

By the time I took this photograph, Ensignbus had taken over Guide Friday, and with it Cambridge's route 007. Former Ipswich Buses Dennis Falcon E1126 KDX is seen at Cambridge station in the spring of 2003.

Stagecoach Viscount Leyland Olympian 16588 (S588 BCE) is seen departing Cambridge on the lengthy X7 to Peterborough in the spring of 2003.

Burtons Mercedes 0814D (S103 VBJ) is seen on the contracted route 17 to Newmarket in the spring of 2003.

One of a few Volvo B6s transferred into the Cambus fleet (all of which outlived the fourteen that were new to Cambus), L837 CDG is seen in Cambridge city centre in the spring of 2003.

Morley's Leyland Titan CUL 92Y is seen in the snow at Whittlesey on 31 January 2003. This bus was new to London Transport as T92.

One of forty MAN 18.220s with Alexander bodywork delivered new to Stagecoach in Cambridge in November 2001, 22318 (AE51 RYU) is at Cambridge station on 30 May 2003.

Four of the fourteen Volvo B6s new to Cambus were snapped up by Regal Busways. L660 MFL is seen in Chelmsford while working the 52 in the autumn of 2004.

Stagecoach Cambus Leyland Olympian 506 (F506 NJE) is seen at Cambridge station in the summer of 2003. These Olympians retained their blue seating throughout their long lives with the Cambridgeshire fleets.

Stagecoach Cambus Volvo Olympian P812 GMU is seen in Cambridge on 25 August 2005. This bus would have been transferred to the Cambus fleet in 2001 in LT red, so it would have received its striped livery not long before the Stagecoach Group changed its livery in the autumn of 2001.

Ensignbus Metrobus A646 BCN is seen at Cambridge station on the 007 on 25 August 2005.

Stagecoach Dennis Trident 17053 (T653 KPU) was the 'pool vehicle' for Cambridge Park and Ride and so wore a fawn livery so it could be used on any of the five P&R routes. It is seen here on 26 August 2005.

Stagecoach MAN 18.220 22060 (KV53 FAK) at Cambridge railway station on 25 August 2005.

New to Yorkshire Rider, First Essex Dennis Dart M219 VWW is seen in Chelmsford on 27 August 2005. This was during the time that Chelmsford bus station was being rebuilt, so services were terminating and starting in the surrounding streets.

A441 UVV was one of two Mk 2 Metrobuses delivered new to London Transport for vehicle evaluation trials in the early 1980s. Now owned by Ensignbus, it was used for a while on the 007 in Cambridge. It is now preserved by Ensignbus.

Morley's Leyland Titan KYV 358X is seen in Whittlesey on Friday 16 September 2005.

Stagecoach Dennis Dart 32758 (L758 VNL) is seen in the Fen Ditton area of Cambridge on 4 October 2005.

On a few Sundays in the summer of 2006, Blue Triangle ran free bus services on two routes in Essex using vintage London vehicles. On 16 July 2006, Routemaster coaches RCL2260 (CUV 260C) and RT3062 (KXW 171) are seen in Braintree Bus Park.

Leyland Olympian H474 CEG is seen for the third time in this book, this time in the Stagecoach 'rolling ball' livery, while working one of the Cambridge Park and Ride services on Saturday 22 July 2006.

On Monday 30 April 2007, Stagecoach Optare Solo 47351 (AE06 TWV) is seen at Fulbourn Tesco's on the 16 and 17 from Buchan Street to Newmarket via Cambridge city centre, Teversham, and Great and Little Wilbraham. Previously operated by Burton under contract to Cambridgeshire County Council, the 16 and 17 had recently been registered as a commercial service by Stagecoach when I took this photograph and was generally operated by new Optare Solos. This history of this route goes back to Eastern Counties days when it was the 114 from Cambridge to Newmarket. Unfortunately, the villages on these routes do not make ideal bus operating territory due to high levels of car ownership; as a result, the 16 and 17 gradually withered away.

First Essex Dennis Dart 46822 (L822 OPU) is seen in Braintree Bus Park on town service 21. This service was later extended north to Halstead for a while before being cut back to being just a Braintree town service, and was then eventually withdrawn by First. This bus was new to Eastern National as 822. In 1994 it was under Badgerline ownership for about a year before the formation of FirstBus.

Excel Dennis Dart (EU56 GVG) is seen resting in Braintree Bus Park before venturing out on the very indirect market day service to Great Dunmow in the spring of 2008.

Stansted Transit MAN 14.220 AE08 DLF is seen in the picturesque Essex village of Finchingfield on 17 June 2008.

First Eastern Counties K489 EUX was China Motor Bus LM9 (FW 2788) and was imported by First Group in 2000, becoming fleet number 30105 when the fleet was numbered into the national scheme. All ten LM class buses stayed together, initially in Ashton-under-Lyne, then Manchester's Queens Road, then Glasgow's Parkhead and finally in Great Yarmouth. It is seen in Lowestoft on 21 June 2008.

One of five Leyland-bodied Leyland Olympians built in Workington and purchased by Eastern Counties, J623 BVG was seen in Beccles on Saturday 21 June 2008. It is now running as fleet number 34973. The bodywork is very similar to the ECW bodywork built for many Olympians in Lowestoft prior to the closure of the ECW factory in 1987.

Very much representing typical vehicles in the Stagecoach Cambridge fleet at the time are Dennis Trident 18339 (AE55 DJZ) and MAN 18.220 22459 (S459 OFT), seen on 26 June 2008. The Tridents were new to the Cambridge fleet and spent most of their time on the Citi1 between Arbury and Fulbourn, although they did occasionally stray onto other routes. The MAN 18.220 was typical of the fleet at the time, although this particular one was transferred south from the Stagecoach Busways fleet.

Stansted Transit Dennis Dart SLF KB53 VDP is seen in Braintree Bus Park in 2008 on the local 34A route operated under contract to Essex County Council. Not long after I took this photograph the 34/34A passed to Hedingham Omnibus. Due to cutbacks, it has since been withdrawn. Stansted Transit went into administration in June 2009.

First Eastern Counties Leyland Olympian 34952 (G49 XLO), new to London Buslines, is seen in Carlton Colville on 13 September 2008.

Following the collapse of Stansted Transit in 2009, the 133 was briefly operated by Excel Passenger Logistics, mainly using Dennis Darts, although on 24 September 2009 Scania N113/ East Lancs F712 LFG is seen at Braintree Bus Park awaiting departure to Stansted Airport. This bus was new to Brighton & Hove in 1989.

The 133 passed within the TGM Group to Network Colchester. On 16 October 2009, Dennis Dart S312 JUA is seen in the London livery version of TGM's parent company, Arriva. Not long after this picture was taken this bus was converted to single-door configuration and received Network Colchester livery.

Essex County Bus was a short-lived operator formed from the ashes of Stansted Transit. It launched cross-Chelmsford town service C42 in competition with First Essex route 42. Optare Excel V939 VUB is seen at Broomfield Hospital alongside First Essex Dennis Dart 42486 (SM03 WMX) on 19 October 2009.

Also at Broomfield Hospital on 19 October 2009 is Essex County Bus Optare Excel V937 VUB.

New to Meteor, Essex County Bus Optare Solo T415 OUB is seen in Barnard Road in Galleywood, Chelmsford, while working the C42 on 19 October 2009.

Regal Busways Dennis Dart 602 (YN04 PZZ) is seen opposite the now closed St John's Hospital in Chelmsford on the Essex County Council-contracted route 14 to Wickford on 15 March 2010.

Regal Busways Optare Solo 202 (YJ56 AOT) is seen in Braintree Bus Park, operating the Essex County Council-contracted 34 to Great Notley on 26 June 2010. This route has since been discontinued.

First Essex operated a large fleet of long-wheelbase Optare Solos. One of these, 53139 (EU54 BNJ), is on layover in Braintree Bus Park when seen on 28 June 2010.

Hedingham Omnibus Dennis Dart L325 (EX02 RYR) is seen basking in the early summer sunshine on layover at Braintree Bus Park on 29 June 2010.

First Essex Volvo B7R 66802 (MX05 CCK) is seen in Braintree Bus Park on the recently extended 70 from Colchester to Chelmsford via Braintree on 4 July 2010.

Network Colchester Dennis Dart SN54 HWY is seen in Braintree on Carnival Day, 23 July 2010.

Strathclyde ordered fifty-two Leyland Olympians in 1992 as long-term replacements for the buses lost in the Larkfield fire, and these started to arrive in July 1993. All had low-height Alexander R-type bodies, allowing them to be used on the 66 group of routes from Larkfield Depot. Now First Essex 31198, L163 UNS is seen in Braintree Bus Park on the 70 from Colchester to Chelmsford. The predecessor to First Essex, Eastern National never bought any new double-deckers after privatisation, and First Essex has never received new double-deckers.

Stagecoach Dennis Dart SLF P564 APM appears for a second time in this book. Originally loaned as a demonstrator to Stagecoach Cambus in 1996, hence the Guildford registration, it was purchased by Stagecoach the following year. Seen in Peterborough on 23 October 2010, it was later transferred to Leamington Spa and was withdrawn in 2015.

On 23 October 2010, Bristol FLF JAH 553D is seen for the third time in this book. This time it is in Oundle while working a diagram from Peterborough to mark the occasion of its final day based at Peterborough before being transferred to Kettering.

Stagecoach Dennis Enviro 400 19576 (AE10 BWJ) is seen at Cambridge railway station on the 1 from Fulbourn to Arbury (previously the 5 up to 2001) on 24 March 2011. This whole area has altered almost to the point of being unrecognisable in the years since I took this photograph.

Also taken on 24 March 2011 was this picture of Network Colchester Dennis Dart 521 (SN54 HWZ), which was seen in Braintree Bus Park on what was its usual haunt at the time – the 133 to Stansted Airport. At the time of writing this route is normally worked by 07-registered Volvo B7RLEs, but Darts do still make the occasional appearance.

First Essex Dennis Dart SN03 WMX makes another appearance in this book, this time on layover at Braintree Bus Park on 3 April 2011.

On 30 April 2011, Regal Busways MAN NL273F (RG09 BUS) is seen at Braintree Bus Park on the Saturday contracted service 89 to Great Yeldham. During the week this route was operated commercially by Hedingham.

Despite wearing route branding for cross-Colchester town service 2, Network Colchester Dennis Dart 513 (HX51 LRL) is resting at Braintree Bus Park between turns on the 133 to Stansted Airport on Saturday 30 April 2011.

Hedingham Alexander Dennis Enviro 400 L386 (SN10 CCV) is seen at Braintree Bus Park on 28 July 2011, having just arrived on the 89 from Great Yeldham. This route has since been extended from the Bus Park to the railway station.

Regal Busways Dennis Dart 701 (AE55 EHM) is seen in Braintree Bus Park on 30 July 2011. This bus was later sold to Ensignbus.

Regal Busways Dennis Dart 515 (P392 LPS) is captured in the picturesque Essex village of Little Baddow on the Essex County Council-contracted 31A on Saturday 13 August 2011. This bus was new to Stagecoach as 32392.

Hedingham Dennis Dart L350 (EU56 FLN) is seen out of service heading along Victoria Road on 19 August 2011. This scene is now much changed as the Post Office sorting office behind the bus, completed in 1976, has been demolished and at the time of writing is cleared land that is about to be built on as a residential development. Sadly, the model shop in the image has also closed.

Flagfinders were running this very early Dennis Dart with Carlyle bodywork on the free shuttle bus between Braintree Bus Park and Braintree Freeport right up until the contract for the route passed to Regal in late 2010. This bus was new to R&I Coaches in July 1990 for LRT-tendered routes in London and is seen on 25 September 2011.

In the summer of 2011 the 133 was extended from Braintree to Colchester to replace the withdrawn X22. At the same time a small fleet of route-branded Scania Omnicity single-deckers was allocated to it, and YN53 GGP is seen in Braintree Bus Park on 19 February 2012. These buses were ousted from the 133 by 07-registered Volvo B7RLEs in 2013.

Since 4 March 2013, and up until the time of writing, the 133 has been worked by Volvo B7RLEs transferred from the Arriva Kent & Surrey fleet, which initially received a special livery for working the route. 632 (GN07 AVE) is seen in Colchester on 23 April 2013.

By the time I took this photograph there weren't many step-entrance buses left in the First Essex fleet. Dennis Dart 46158 (N958 CPU) is seen in Braintree on 2 September 2013.

Hedingham Volvo B7TL L330 (EU53 MVZ) is seen on layover in Braintree Bus Park on 25 September 2013. Hedingham became part of the Go-Ahead Group on 5 March 2012.

Regal Busways Dennis Dart 601 (YN04 PZY) is seen at Braintree Bus Park on 30 October 2013. It is difficult to believe that this very scruffy looking bus was only nine years old when I took this picture.

Hedingham Volvo B10B L301 (S376 MVP) is also seen at Braintree Bus Park on 30 October 2013.

Regal Busways Dennis Dart Y252 NLK was still in the livery of its previous owner, Metroline, when captured in Chelmsford on 20 January 2014. When part of the Metroline fleet this bus was allocated fleetnumber DLM152.

First Eastern Counties Volvo B9TL 36175 (BD11 CFZ) is seen at Norwich Thorpe railway station on 2 February 2014 in an early version of route-branding livery for a Norwich city service.

Very shortly before its withdrawal and scrapping, First Essex Volvo Olympian 34014 (P554 EFL) is seen in Colchester on 3 February 2014. This bus was new to Stagecoach Cambus as 554 as part of a large batch leased by the operator in 1996/7 to replace elderly Bristol VRTs in the Cambus and Viscount fleets. When the lease expired, they were snapped up by several operators.

For quite a few years Network Colchester operated the 70 between Colchester and Braintree on Sundays under contract to Essex County Council. Former Armchair/Metroline Dennis Trident KN52 NEF is seen at Braintree on Sunday 16 February 2014.

First Essex Dennis Trident 33087 (LN51 GMO) is seen arriving at the stand at Braintree Bus Park on Monday 24 February 2014 on the 70 from Colchester to Chelmsford. By this time the 70 was the only route to serve Chelmsford (other than schools) that could be operated by double-deckers. This was due to it being the only route not to pass under the railway bridge in Duke Street, where the road surface had recently been raised, thus reducing the permitted height of vehicles passing underneath.

Network Colchester Dennis Dart S303 JUA is looking very smart in this image taken in Colchester on 24 February 2014. This bus was new to Arriva London and was later sold to Panther Travel of Essex, who re-registered it BIG 7006.

Regal Busways Optare 209 (YJ60 KHA) is seen in Duke Street, Chelmsford, on Wednesday 5 March 2014.

First Essex Volvo B10B 62139 (X618 NSS) in Aberdeen Corporation heritage livery is seen in Braintree, loading for the 132 to Witham, on Tuesday 10 March 2015.

Stephensons buses have become a very familiar sight in the Braintree and Witham area since retrenchment by First Essex. Dennis Enviro200 EU64 CVT is seen in Braintree Bus Park on the Essex County Council-contracted route 9 to Great Bardfield via Shalford and Finchingfield on Friday 20 March 2015.

Regal Busways Dennis Trident V761 HBY is seen in Braintree on the free shuttle to Freeport Shopping Centre on Friday 20 March 2015. This bus was new to Metroline as TP61.

First Essex Dennis Dart 42447 (R447 CCV) is seen on layover at Braintree Bus Park before heading off to Witham on the 132 on Monday 24 March 2014.

Dennis Dart L404 (W791 VMV) was new to Brighton & Hove and had been recently transferred to Hedingham when seen in Braintree on 22 July 2014, still in B&H livery but with Hedingham fleetnames.

First Eastern Counties Dennis Trident 32107 (LT02 ZCX) is captured here in Castle Meadow, Norwich, on 18 August 2014.

Go-Ahead subsidiary Konectbus Optare Solo 950 (AU07 KMM) is seen in Norwich on 18 August 2014, still in the livery of sister company Anglian Bus.

Formerly of Reading, Sanders Scania L94 316 (YN05 GXX) is seen in Cromer on the 44A to Sheringham on 19 August 2014.

Sanders Optare Solo 211 (YK04 KWB) is also seen in Cromer on 19 August 2014.

Hedingham Dennis Dart 291 (EU06 KCX) is seen in Braintree on soon-to-be-withdrawn town service 34 on 3 March 2015. Although at first glance the change of ownership in 2012 does not appear to have had any effect on the appearance of this bus, it is interesting to note that the large traditional Hedingham fleetnumbers have been discontinued.

First Essex Volvo B10B 62195 (X689 ADK) with Wright Renown bodywork was transferred south from Aberdeen. It is seen here at Braintree Bus Park on 2 May 2015.

Seen on 16 May 2015, Regal Busways Dennis Dart 613 (W701 BFV) was new to Stagecoach Ribble, one of a pair bought for local contract work in the Clitheroe area. The other was registered W701 BFV. Both transferred with Stagecoach's East Lancs operations to Blazefield in 2001, later being transferred away from Clitheroe when that depot closed following the loss of the contracts. This bus was a Keighley-based bus before being sold to Regal. It was not unusual at all for Regal to press a bus into service still in its previous owner's livery.

Route-branded for Colchester town service 1, Network Colchester Dennis Dart SN54 HFX is working Sunday service 352 between Halstead and Chelmsford when spotted on Sunday 7 June 2015.

Ipswich Buses Dennis Dart 139 (Y271 FJN) was new to Stagecoach London as 34271. Now with Ipswich Buses, it is seen in Shotley on Monday 22 June.

First Volvo B7R 66982 is in the Ipswich version of First's livery when seen in Ipswich town centre on Monday 22 June 2015.

Stagecoach Norfolk Green Optare Solo MX56 ABO was still in Norfolk Green livery when I photographed it in Wells-next-the-Sea on 30 August 2015.

Stagecoach Norfolk Green Optare Solo SR 48023 (YJ15 ANR) is also seen in Wells-next-the-Sea on 30 August 2015.

Stagecoach Norfolk Green Optare Solo 47904 (YJ09 LBA) is captured in Wells-next-the-Sea on 30 August 2015.

One of a few Volvo B10Bs operated by Network Colchester, W901 UJM, along with the rest of the Colchester fleet, has received a national Arriva fleetnumber, this one being 3830. The last few remaining Volvo B10Bs were withdrawn not long after I took this photograph, on 29 September 2015.

Working the Essex County Council-contracted 70 Sunday service on 4 October 2015 is Network Colchester Scania OmniDekka YN06 TFZ. Not long after this picture was taken, the 70 Sunday service was extended from Braintree to Chelmsford and passed to First Essex.

Still in Fastrack livery for services in Kent, Arriva Volvo B7R 3815 (GN07 AVB) is seen at Braintree, working on the 133 to Stansted Airport on 7 October 2015.

Hedingham Volvo Olympian R629 MNU didn't have long to go when I took this picture at Witham railway station on 12 October 2015. It is seen waiting to depart to Tollesbury on an afternoon working on the 91, which Hedingham inherited with the Osborne's business when Hedingham took over the operator in 1997. Hedingham closed the Tollesbury Depot in 2016.

Network Colchester Volvo B7R 3818 (GN07 AVE) is seen departing Braintree Bus Park on a late morning departure to Stansted Airport on 12 October 2015. These comfortable buses are very well suited to the lengthy 133 and at the time of writing are still working the majority of journeys on this route, although now in standard Arriva livery without route branding.